MONSTER TRUCKS
MEGA MACHINES
in 3D

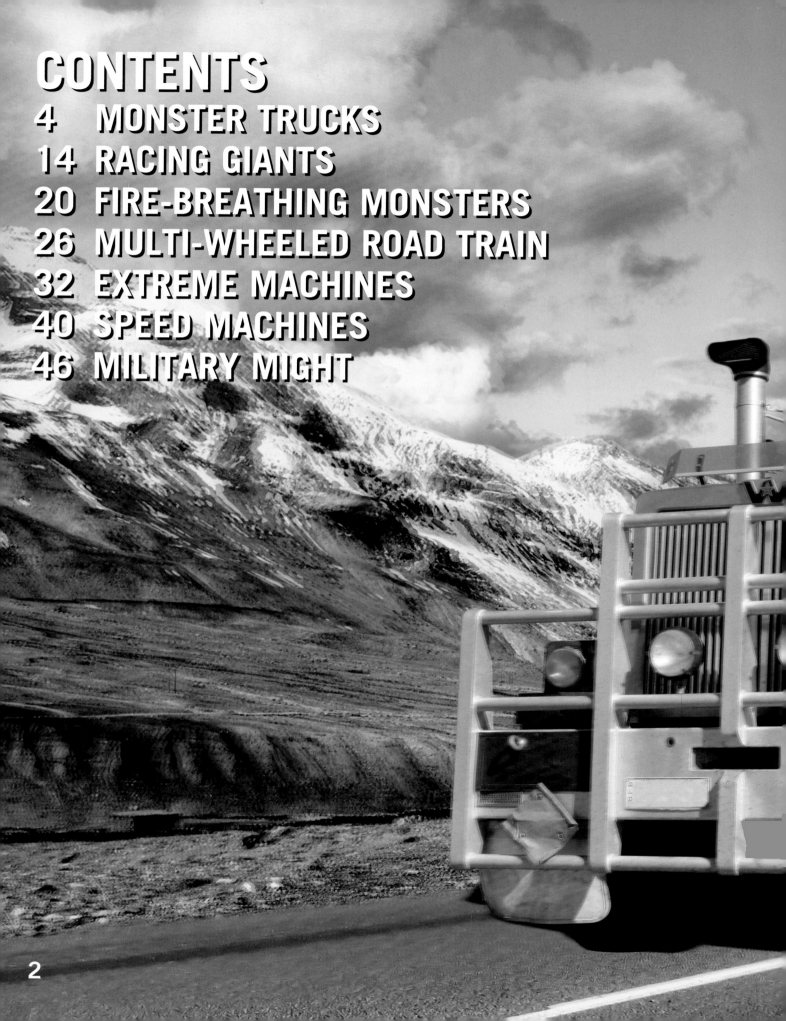

CONTENTS

Fasten your seatbelt and prepare for an amazing 3D journey with some of the world's most astounding mega machines. Put on your 3D glasses and watch these mighty trucks coming right at you!

MONSTER
TRUCKS

Bob Chandler
became the
first person to
drive over cars
in his famous
monster truck
called Bigfoot.

A monster truck is a spectacular pickup truck modified with enormous wheels and suspension. These mechanical mutants are popular attractions at motor sports events – and often take turns at car crushing!

MONSTER TRUCKS

These towering trucks have wheels that are 65 inches high (1.65 metres): as tall as an average person.

Most monster truck bodies are made of fiberglass or carbon fiber, which is light but strong.

The body of a monster truck gives it its identity. Highly decorated and certainly grabs the audience's attention!

The famous Red Dragon is not exactly economical: with a monstrous 1300 horsepower engine, it only gets 55 yards (50 metres) to the gallon!

MONSTER
TRUCKS

If monster trucks are your thing, get yourself to a Pit Party at a Monster Jam event!

9

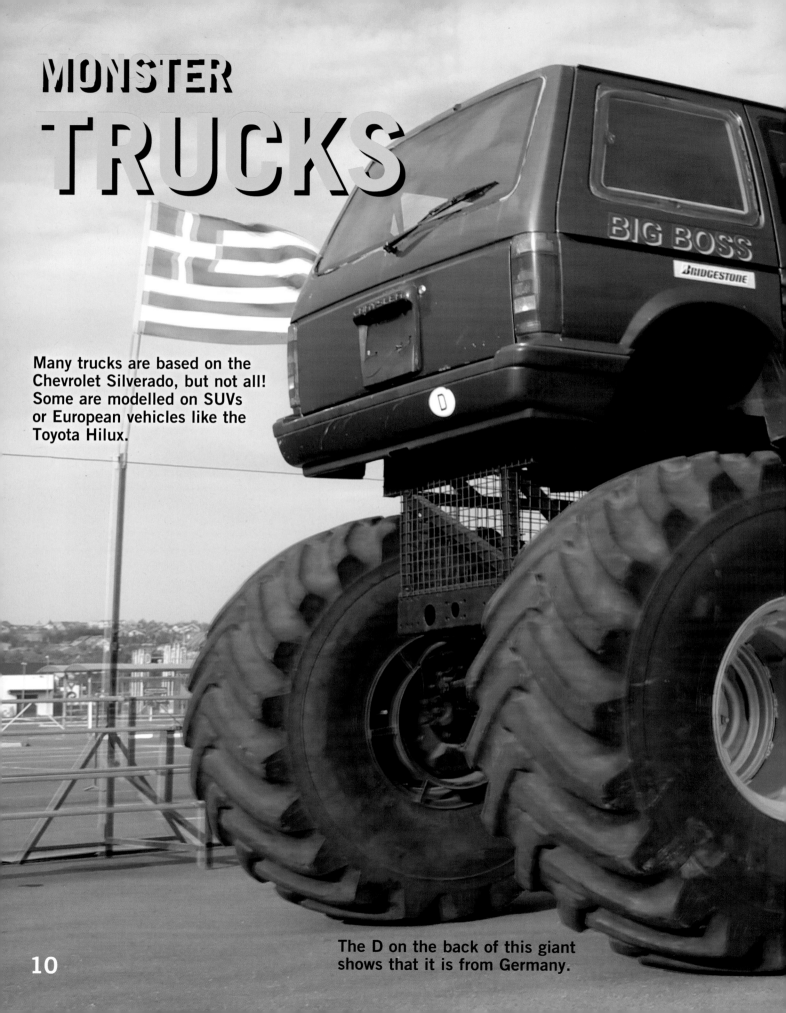

MONSTER TRUCKS

Many trucks are based on the Chevrolet Silverado, but not all! Some are modelled on SUVs or European vehicles like the Toyota Hilux.

BIG BOSS

BRIDGESTONE

The D on the back of this giant shows that it is from Germany.

Long-stroke suspension gives more clearance over rough ground and all kinds of obstacles. It also gives a bigger bounce!

If you're giving your monster truck a huge monster name, what better than naming it after an enormous, iconic, destructive giant?!

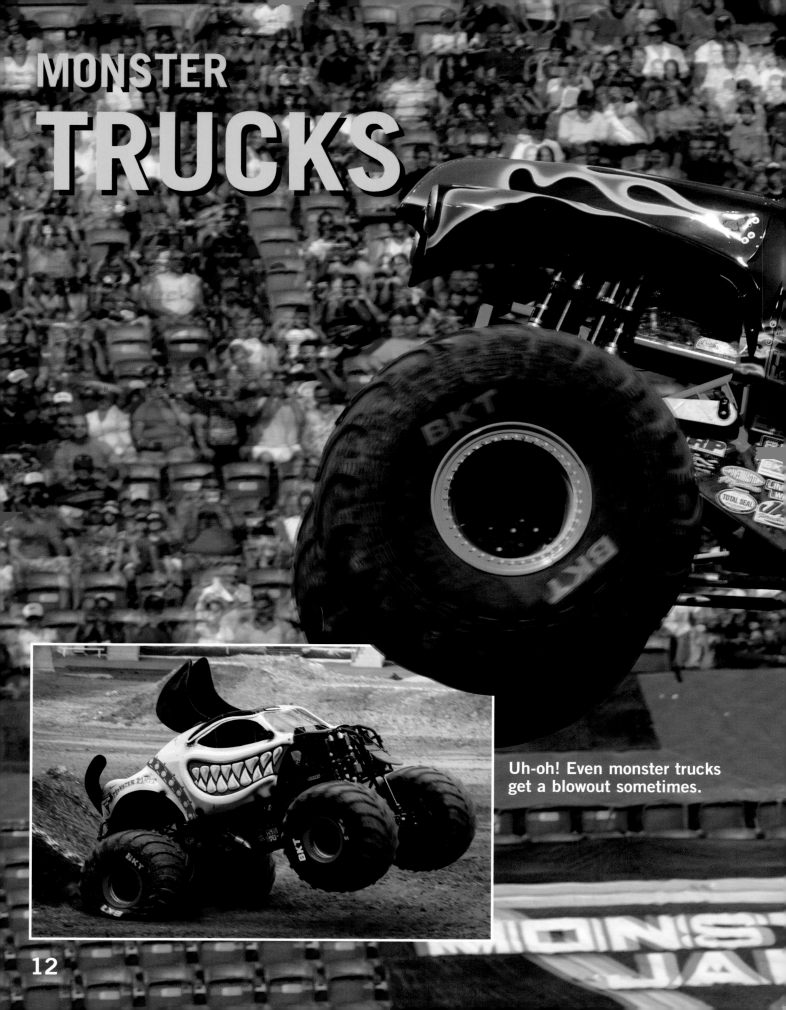

MONSTER TRUCKS

Uh-oh! Even monster trucks get a blowout sometimes.

Charlie Pauken smashed onto the scene in his Grave Digger truck. What a crazy vehicle!

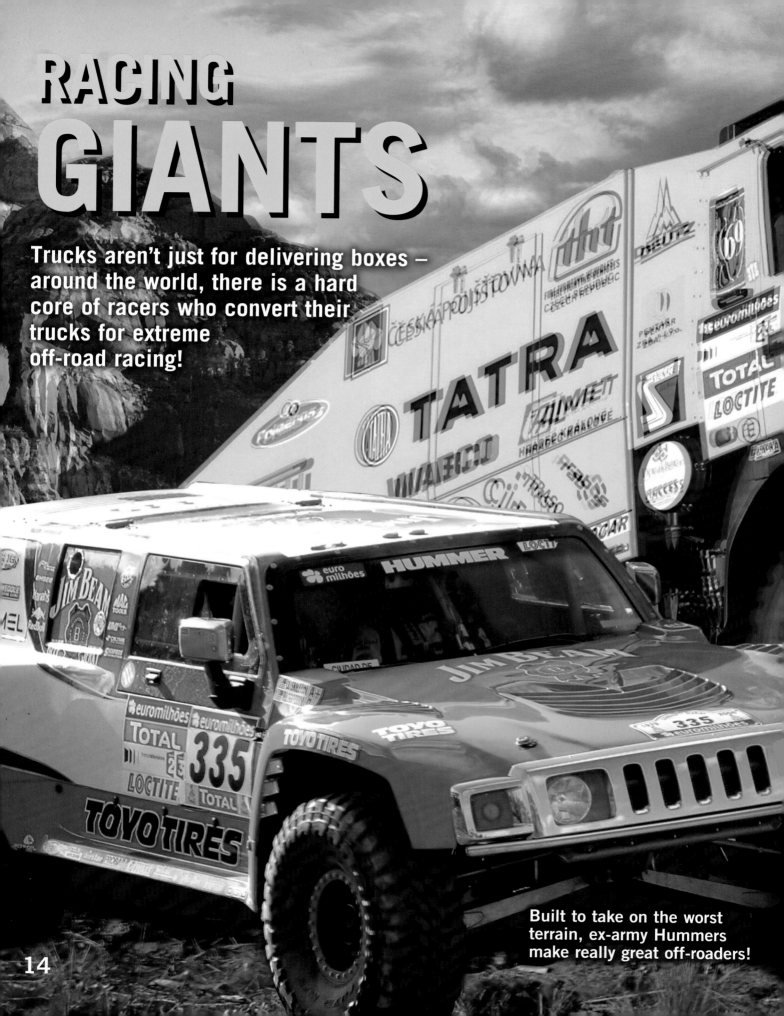

RACING GIANTS

Trucks aren't just for delivering boxes – around the world, there is a hard core of racers who convert their trucks for extreme off-road racing!

Built to take on the worst terrain, ex-army Hummers make really great off-roaders!

Pickup dirt racing is really scary and not for the faint-hearted!

Off-road truck racing is very popular in Asia and Eastern Europe – like these guys getting down and dusty in the Ukraine!

RACING
GIANTS

Truck racing began
way back in 1979
in Atlanta, Georiga.

RACING GIANTS

Racing trucks come from all over the world. Huge and powerful, they generally weigh in around 5 tons.

Truck racing has to be seen to be believed. A track-side view is an exhilarating experience!

19

FIRE-BREATHING MONSTERS

High octane fuels can propel vehicles at phenomenal speeds – but not without considerable danger! A nitromethane mixture is often used in drag racing, but can result in a very hot situation!

Get ready for blast off!

Jet power + truck power + too much
pedal = Call the fire department!

Fortunately, the flames on this
customised 1950s Ford pickup
are just for show!

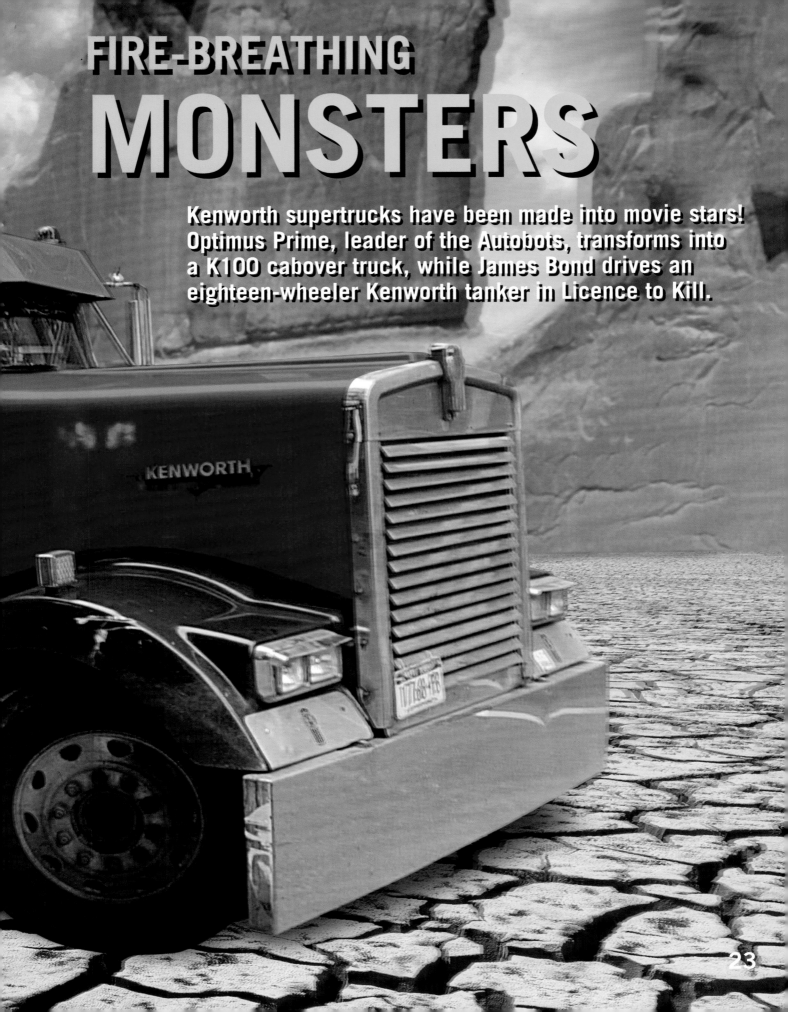

FIRE-BREATHING
MONSTERS

Kenworth supertrucks have been made into movie stars! Optimus Prime, leader of the Autobots, transforms into a K100 cabover truck, while James Bond drives an eighteen-wheeler Kenworth tanker in Licence to Kill.

FIRE-BREATHING MONSTERS

If you feel the need for speed, then Shockwave is the truck for you. A record-breaking beast, it clocks over 370 mph (600 kph). Afterburners add to the power and thrust, just like those in a fighter plane.

SHOCKWAVE
At those speeds, no wonder it needs parachutes to slow down!

MULTI-WHEELED
ROAD TRAINS

Multi-trailered road trains are an awesome sight! Catch them trucking across remote areas of North and South America and Australia. They don't just pull one trailer, they take three, weighing up to 200 tons. That's one almighty road trip!

A road train carrying cattle thunders across Australia's outback.

Check out the cargo on this mighty road train. Destination: many, many miles away!

For haulage from forest to timberyard, you need a long logging truck.

27

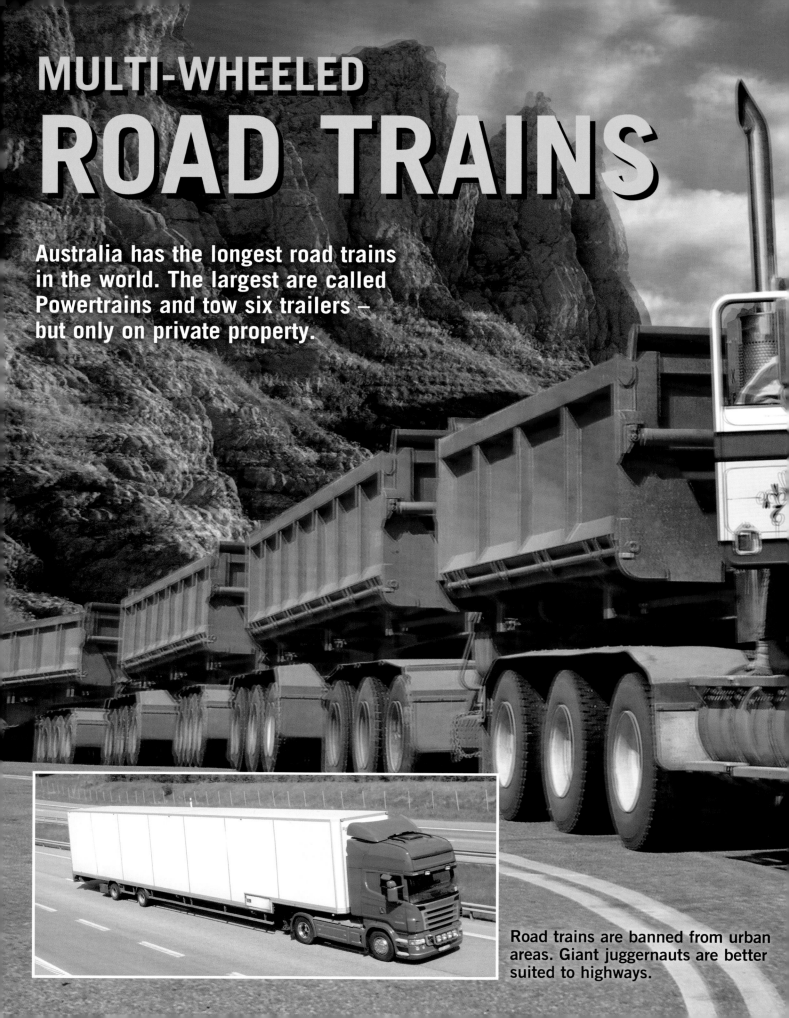

MULTI-WHEELED
ROAD TRAINS

Australia has the longest road trains in the world. The largest are called Powertrains and tow six trailers – but only on private property.

Road trains are banned from urban areas. Giant juggernauts are better suited to highways.

MULTI-WHEELED ROAD TRAINS

ROAD TRAINS

50 METRES LONG

Once these giants get moving, they are extremely difficult to stop. Car drivers beware: don't cut them up or you'll likely end up squished.

EXTREME
MACHINES

No terrain is too tough for the most monstrous trucks. Snow, ice, mountains, deserts, mines – here are a few machines that survive where all the others fail...

This tough truck is built to stand up to just about anything – very handy if you live somewhere remote, muddy or mountainous!

EXTREME
MACHINES

Earthmovers and bulldozers are used in mining and construction. It takes a skilled operator to use them, especially the very biggest ones.

Mining machines are amazing feats of engineering, they are some of the biggest vehicles you will ever see. The largest haul trucks can move 400 tons of sand, gravel or dirt.

Haul trucks, or dump trucks, are so huge that the driver climbs up ladders to get to the cab and into the driving seat.

EXTREME
MACHINES

The biggest mining saws have a blade the size of a four-storey building. It takes around 20 people to operate!

Clearing the ground uses some of the biggest machines of them all, such as saws and bucket wheel excavators (BWEs). The largest BWEs are some of the heaviest land vehicles ever made.

SPEED
MACHINES

Top speeds and a huge adrenaline rush? This must be Formula One racing! It's fast and furious but also competitive, dangerous, and extremely expensive...

The fastest cars can go from zero to 60 mph in just 2.6 seconds and reach top speeds of well over 200 mph. It's not just about the acceleration though: they can also brake from 100 mph to zero in four seconds.

SPEED MACHINES

Top riders take corners fast and low so that their knee almost touches the track.

Travelling at top speeds on just two wheels might just be the definition of crazy. These mega-motorbikes are based on road bikes but modified to make them lighter and much, much faster.

SPEED
MACHINES

Don't be fooled by the slimline body and those tiny front wheels. This car is super fast. Top Fuel Drag cars are way, way faster than F1 cars, reaching speeds in excess of 300 mph.

Blink and you'll miss it — these races are long, low, and lightning-fast.

Fancy a BIG race? Get behind the wheel of these off-roaders and see how they hug the track. They aren't 4 x 4s, they're 6 x 6s!

44

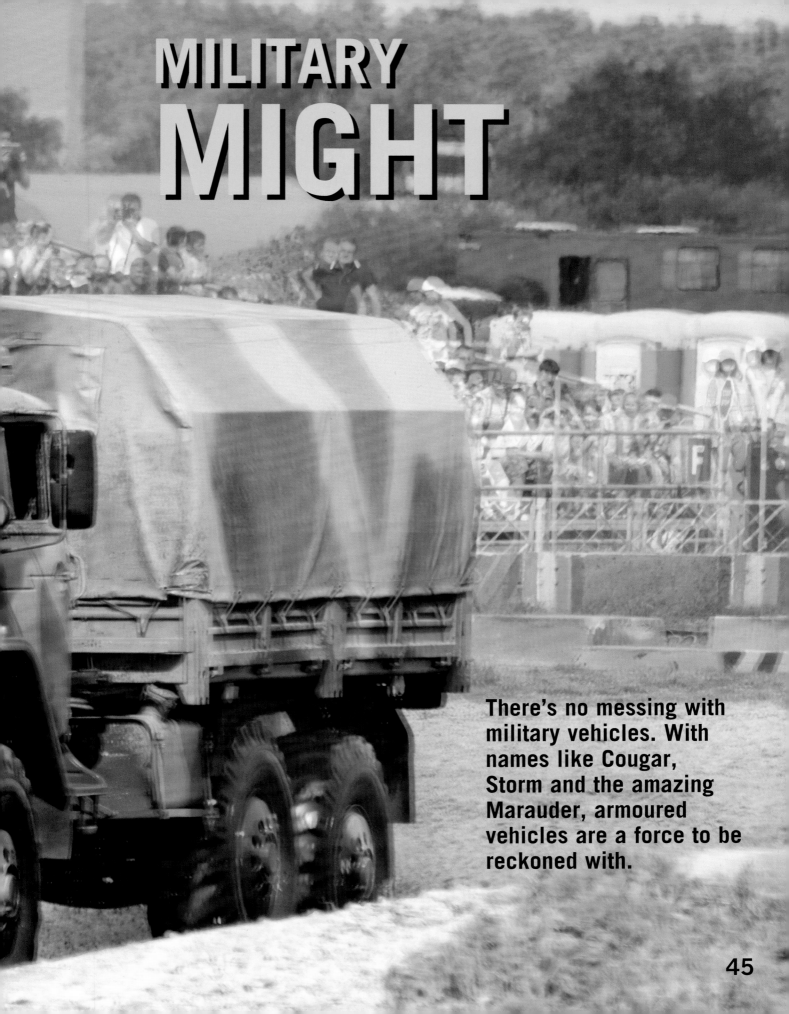

MILITARY MIGHT

There's no messing with military vehicles. With names like Cougar, Storm and the amazing Marauder, armoured vehicles are a force to be reckoned with.

MILITARY MIGHT

This MLR (Multiple Launch Rocket) system certainly has some firepower. It has 40 tubes to launch mobile ground rockets far into the distance.

If you think this is awesome, imagine four of them joined together. That's the world's biggest cradle launcher, made for the United Arab Emirates army, which has a total of 240 tubes on a trailer carrying four launchers.

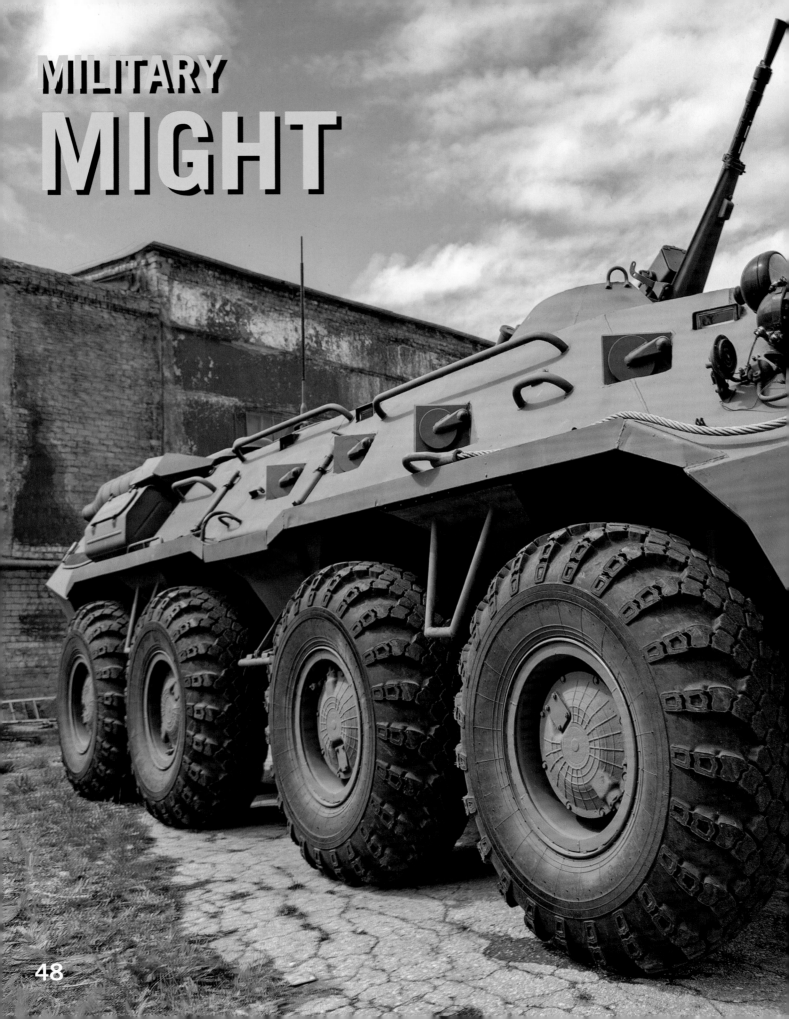

MILITARY
MIGHT